PETS PLUS

Horses

Sally Morgan

A+

Smart Apple Media

Published by Smart Apple Media, an imprint of Black Rabbit Books
P.O. Box 3263, Mankato, Minnesota 56002
www.blackrabbitbooks.com

Printed in the United States of America at Corporate Graphics, Inc. North Mankato, Minnesota.

Published by arrangement with the Watts Publishing Group LTD, London.

Library of Congress Cataloging-in-Publication Data
Morgan, Sally, 1957-
 Horses / Sally Morgan.
    p. cm. -- (Pets plus)
 Includes index.
 Summary: "Describes different types of horses, and how to care for and train a pet horse. Wild horses, as
well as horse communication are described to help the reader further understand natural horse
behavior"--Provided by publisher.
 ISBN 978-1-59920-702-5 (library binding)
 1. Horses--Juvenile literature. I. Title.
 SF302.M665 2013
 636.1--dc23
                              2011040183

Created by Taglines Creative Ltd: www.taglinescreative.com
Author: Sally Morgan
Series designer: Hayley Cove
Editor: Jean Coppendale

Picture credits
t=top b=bottom l=left r=right m=middle
Cover: logo Olga/Shutterstock; horses heads Dhoxax/Shutterstock; wild horses
chantal de brijne/Shutterstock; Contents and top of spreads: horse, Shutterstock/
EricLam; Przewalski, Shutterstock/Pandapaw; p4 Shutterstock/Loflo69; p5t Shutterstock/
Lenkadan, 5b istock/The Biggles; p6 Alamy/Sally and Richard Greenhill; p7t Shutterstock/
Sonya Etchison, 7b Shutterstock/Nikoner; p8 Shutterstock/Groomec; p9t Shutterstock/
Holbox and Microcosmos, 9b Michael Westhoff/iStockphoto (saddle), Shutterstock/
Cathleen A Clapper (other items); p10, 11, 12 Ecoscene/Angela Hampton;
p13t Shutterstock/Anita Huszti, 13b Shutterstock/ Jeff Banke; p14
Shutterstock/Zuzule; p15t Ecoscene/Angela Hampton, 15b
Shutterstock/Jennyt; p16 Shutterstock/Christian Mueller; p17 life cycle
1 Shutterstock/Melissa Dockstader, life cycle 2 Ecoscene/Angela Hampton,
lifecycle 3 Shutterstock/Alex White, 17b Shutterstock/Winthrop Brookhouse;
p18 Shutterstock/Groomec; p19t Shutterstock/Makarova Viktoria, 19b
Shutterstock/Dr Ajay Kumar; p20 Shutterstock/Lebanmax; p21t
Shutterstock/Harry March, 21b Ecoscene/Angela Hampton; p22
Shutterstock/ Alixia Khruscheva; p23t Shutterstock/Paige White,
23b Ecoscene/Angla Hampton; p24 Shutterstock/Cynoclub;
p25t Shutterstock/Tamara Didenko, 25b Shutterstock/
Villion van Niekerk; p26l Shutterstock/
Graham@graphiczone, 26r Wiki/Phil Konstantin;
p27 Wiki/Kersti Nebelsiek; p30 Shutterstock/
Dhoxax; p31 Shutterstock/Chantal de Bruijne

Every attempt has been made to clear copyright on the photographs
used in this book. Should there be any inadvertent omission,
please apply to the publisher for rectification.

PO 1436 / Feb 2012

9 8 7 6 5 4 3 2 1

Contents

The meaning of the words in **bold** can be found in the glossary.

Pet Horses, Wild Horses

Wild horses have been tamed by humans for thousands of years. They help us work, and we ride them for pleasure.

Last Wild Horses

The Przewalski's (*PER-zhih-VAHL-skeez*) horse of Mongolia is the last truly wild horse left in the world. All the other wild horse **breeds** have been **domesticated**. Other wild breeds, such as the **mustang** of North America, the brumby of Australia and the sorraia of Spain and Portugal, are related to horses that escaped from **captivity**, and have lived wild for many years. These are called **feral** horses.

▲ There are only 400 Przewalski's horses living wild in Mongolia and China.

▲ Domestic horses, such as this American paint horse, are trained for competitions.

Work and Ride

Many horses are **bred** to do a certain job. For example, heavy Clydesdale horses are bred to pull wagons and plows. Some horses are bred for people who want to ride for fun and in competitions such as **rodeos** and horse shows.

How Many Hands?

Horses are measured in hands from the ground to the highest point of its **withers**, where the neck meets the back. A hand is 4 in. (10 cm). The smallest horses are ponies. They are usually under 14.2 hands high.

◀ A pony is under 14.2 hands high, while a horse is taller.

Where Can I Learn to Ride?

Learning to ride a horse is exciting and great exercise. But it can be very expensive, and looking after a horse takes up a lot of time.

Learning to Ride

Buying a horse and the riding equipment you will need is very costly. Some riding stables may offer free or reduced price lessons if you help care for the horses. If you want your own horse, you could contact a horse charity to see if you can rescue a horse.

Do It!

When you choose a horse, make sure it is suitable for your riding ability. If you are a beginner, you do not want a horse that gets very excited and enjoys fast gallops.

▼ You can learn how to ride safely at a local riding school.

Stable and Pasture

Not all horses need a stable, but they must have a fenced **paddock**, with a water supply and a shelter where they can lie down in a dry area. Wild horses live in herds, and do not like to be alone. The same is true for pet horses. They should be kept with another horse or pony, or even a sheep or goat. You can keep your horse in a **livery yard**. This is ideal if you cannot visit your horse every day, because other people will be there to look after it.

▲ If you work at a local stable you will learn a lot about horses and how to look after them.

▼ Renting a stable for your horse at a livery yard means it will be with other horses.

Preparing for Your Horse

Before you can own a horse, you will need to get a stable and paddock ready for its arrival, and also buy the equipment that you will need.

Perfect Paddock

The paddock should have good quality grass and a supply of clean water. If you use electric fencing, check that the **fencer** is working. Make sure the paddock does not have any stones or poisonous plants in it. Ask an expert to check out the paddock for you.

Stables

A stable needs to be large enough for your horse to turn around and lie down. Make sure the stable is cleaned out daily, and that there is always fresh bedding, such as straw, on the floor. Your horse will need to be let out into a paddock every day so it can exercise.

▼ Make sure the fence around your paddock is in good condition and not broken or falling down.

Tack

Tack is all the equipment worn by a horse, including the saddle and bridle. A saddle is placed on the back of the horse over a blanket or pad, and strapped in place with the **girth**. The bridle consists of a **halter**, a **bit,** which goes in the horse's mouth, and the reins. You will also need a **lunge line** to exercise your horse. Stables should be able to supply these.

▲ A well-fitting saddle is important, otherwise it will rub your horse's back and cause sores.

Do It!

Checklist—equipment you will need for you and your horse:

- stable or shelter
- tack
- feed tub
- **grooming** brushes and combs
- hoof pick
- pitch fork
- wheelbarrow
- manure fork
- broom
- water bucket or trough

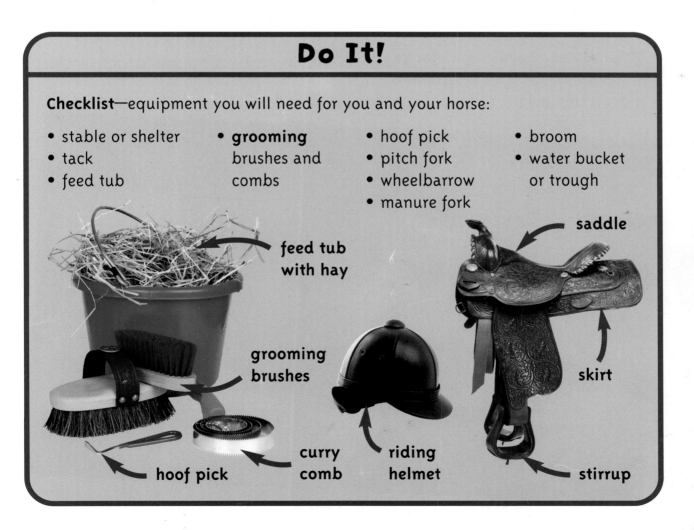

feed tub with hay

saddle

grooming brushes

skirt

hoof pick

curry comb

riding helmet

stirrup

Caring for Your Horse

There is a lot to learn about keeping a horse. You have to feed and water it, groom it, and keep its stable and paddock clean.

Daily Care

Your horse needs to be checked twice a day. On each of your visits, make sure there is plenty of fresh water, give your horse some food, and see if it needs grooming.

▼ Put hay in a haynet or a **manger** so it does not drop on the ground and get trampled.

Horse Food

A pony or horse that is resting can live on grass or hay. But a horse that is being ridden every day needs more food, such as horse pellets. There are many different types of horse pellets. Ask your food supplier for advice.

Mucking Out

A horse needs to have a clean stable. Every day you will need to collect all its droppings and replace the bedding so it has a dry, fresh bed. This is called mucking out.

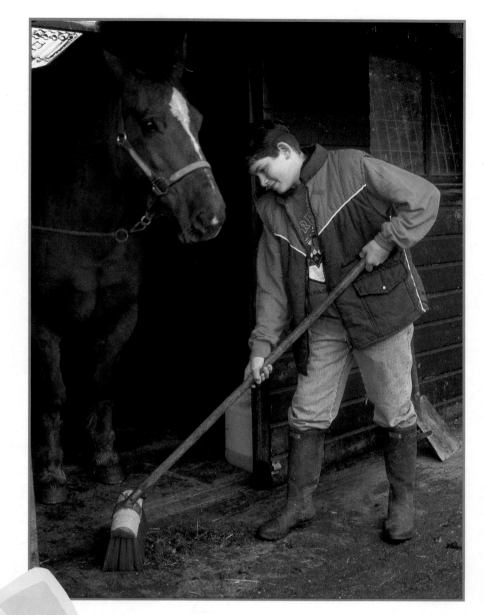

▶ Mucking out is dirty work, so always wash your hands afterwards.

PET POINT

If you are going to ride your horse, make sure you leave at least an hour between feeding and exercise.

Paddock Care

Paddocks have to be kept clean, too. You have to clear up all the droppings, as they stop the grass from growing. You will need to watch how much grass your horse eats, because too much fresh grass in the spring can give your horse **laminitis**.

11

Grooming Your Horse

Grooming your horse will keep its coat clean. At the same time, you can check your horse for injuries and skin problems.

Preparation

Get your grooming equipment ready. You will need:

- curry comb or grooming mitt
- body brush with fairly stiff bristles
- mane and tail comb
- finishing brush with soft bristles
- clean sponge or soft cloth to wipe your horse's face.

Body Brush

Use a curry comb to loosen any dirt, and then a body brush to remove the dirt and dust. Finally, use a soft finishing brush to shine the horse's coat and to brush its head. Use a soft cloth to wipe around your horse's eyes and mouth. A mane comb will get rid of any tangles in its mane and tail.

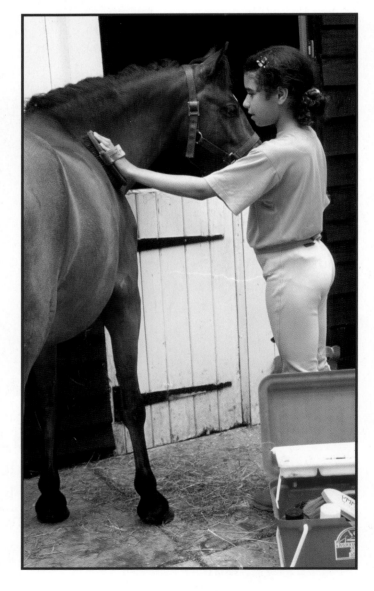

▲ Always brush your horse in the direction that its hair is growing.

▲ In the wild, horses groom each other's backs using their teeth.

Wild Grooming

Wild horses groom each other. Horses cannot reach the hair on their shoulders and back, so other horses groom these areas for them using their front teeth.

Shoeing

Wild horses run on grass, but pet horses walk on hard surfaces, such as roads, so they have to be fitted with shoes to protect their hooves. The hoof grows all the time, so every 4 to 8 weeks you should call a **farrier** to refit the shoes.

Do It!

Always groom your horse before riding because even the smallest bits of dirt under the saddle or girth can cause sores.

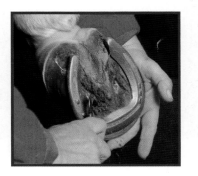

◄ Iron horse shoes protect horses' hooves.

Wild Cousins

Although the only wild horse in the world is the Przewalski's horse, there are many types of feral horses.

Living in Herds

A herd of wild horses is made up of a number of **mares** with their young, and a **stallion**. Some horses, for example Dartmoor ponies and Camargue horses, are semi-feral. This means they live a wild life, but they are owned by people.

Mustangs

Mustangs are descended from Spanish horses that were taken to Mexico for transport and to carry goods. Today they are found mainly in the western United States. They survive well there because there is lots of grass for them to eat.

▲ A herd of feral horses, such as these mustangs, is usually led by a mare. There are large herds of mustangs living in the wild.

Surviving Winter

Ponies in the wild grow a thick coat to keep their bodies warm in the harsh winter months. Pet horses that are stabled are protected from the weather, so they do not grow a thick coat. Also, grooming removes the natural oils that help to protect the horse against cold and wet weather. This means that many pet horses need a blanket in winter to stay warm.

◄ This pet horse (left) has a blanket to wear outside in the winter. But, wild Dartmoor ponies (below) have a thick, shaggy coat to keep them warm.

Colts and Fillies

Female horses are ready to breed when they are about 2 or 3 years old. They are pregnant for almost a year.

Born at Night

Both wild and pet horses give birth mainly at night. It is safer then because **predators** cannot see them so easily. Usually, horses have one **foal**, but sometimes they have twins. Foals are able to stand up within minutes of being born. They have a soft woolly coat, which is replaced by coarser long hairs by the time they are about 2 months old.

◄ A young foal's legs are very long compared to its small body, and it will be able to run about within a few hours of its birth.

Life Cycle

A mare is pregnant for just under 12 months, and she usually has a foal every two years. Once a foal is a year old it is called a yearling. When it is aged between 2 and 4 years, a male is known as a colt, and a female is called a filly. A horse usually lives for 25 to 30 years, but some have lived for more than 60 years.

new-born foal

1-month-old foal suckling

colt running

Staying Close

In the wild, the first few days of a foal's life are risky, and it will stay close to its mother. The mare protects her foal, kicking any predator that comes too close.

The foal's teeth appear within a week, so they can start to nibble grass, although they are still drinking milk. A pet foal feeds on its mother's milk for about four months. In the wild, foals may **suckle** from their mother for as long as a year.

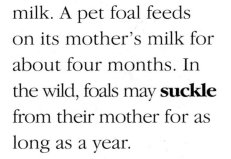

◀ Young wild horses, like this mustang, stay with the herd until they are about 2 years old. Then they leave to join another herd.

Ready to Ride

Young horses have to be trained to use a saddle and bridle. The training starts when they are still foals.

Training

Foals are too young to ride, but they can be trained to wear a halter within days of being born. This means they can be led on a rein, groomed, and checked by a vet. In its first year, a foal should learn words of command and become used to having a blanket on its back. But young horses should not be ridden until they are at least 3 or 4 years old, depending on the type and size of the horse.

PET POINT

You need a lot of patience when training a horse. Never shout at or hit your horse.

▼ Young horses can be trained on a lunge line before they are ridden.

Starting to Ride

To start riding a horse, first a saddle is placed on its back, and when it is happy with this, a person can get on the saddle. Once a horse accepts a rider, the training continues until the horse is safe to ride.

◀ Wild horses (left) love to run and show off. Trained Lipizzaners (below) put on amazing dressage shows and travel around the world.

Dressage

In the wild, horses love to run, jump and kick, and show off to each other. Domesticated horses also like to be active, and **dressage** is a chance for them to show what they can do. Both rider and horse train for many years in order to perform a series of difficult movements.

Running Wild

Wild horses live in herds that roam the plains. Horses like wide open spaces so they can see predators from afar.

Wandering

Horses in the wild have a routine. Much of the day is spent walking and grazing. At some point during the day they walk to water to drink. Nighttime can be dangerous, so the herd gathers together, and the horses sleep for a few hours. Your pet horse will follow a similar routine if it is kept in a paddock.

▼ Feral horses, such as these Camargue horses, drink water from rivers, streams, and ponds.

Underground Vibrations

Horses have sensitive feet that can detect vibrations in the ground. They can tell if there are horses running in the distance, and this can serve as an early warning of danger. If one horse in a herd spots a predator and runs away, the whole herd will run.

▲ Galloping horses act as a warning to other horses in the same area.

Senses

Horses have eyes on the side of their head. This means they can see predators approaching, but they have a **blind spot** right in front of their nose. It is always best to walk and stand to the side of a horse so you do not make it nervous. Horses use their sense of smell to sniff out food and water. They can identify other horses, and even people, from their smell.

◀ Horses have a long, narrow head with big, round eyes placed high on each side.

Your Wild Pet

Your pet horse may live in a stable and graze in a paddock, but it still has a lot in common with its wild cousins.

Rolling Around

Wild horses love to roll on the ground. They often choose a sandy place and roll on their backs to have a good stretch. Usually all the horses in a herd come to the same spot to roll around. Pet horses have a favorite rolling spot, too.

▲ Rolling helps to keep horses healthy by stretching their muscles.

Rolling spreads dirt over the horse's coat, and this helps to stop insects from biting. Horses also like to roll if they are sweaty after a ride to help dry off the sweat.

Soft Touch

Horses are very sensitive to touch, particularly around their eyes, nose, and ears. They use their whiskers to feel objects. Horses can also feel an insect landing on their body and use their tail to swish it away. Horses prefer to be stroked rather than patted. You can bond with your pet by stroking it and getting close to it.

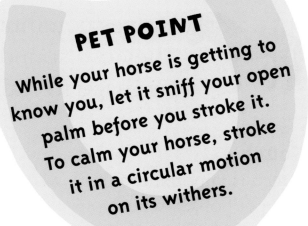

PET POINT

While your horse is getting to know you, let it sniff your open palm before you stroke it. To calm your horse, stroke it in a circular motion on its withers.

◀ Wild horses (left) enjoy nuzzling each other, and your pet horse (bottom) will enjoy a hug.

Horse Talk

Horses communicate in different ways. They use sound, smell, touch, and body language to "talk" to each other.

Touch

Touch is important for both wild and pet horses. When you ride, your legs make contact with the horse. By pressing hard with your legs you can tell a horse to change direction or move faster.

When you pull on the reins, the touch on the mouth tells a horse to stop.

▼ When you are riding, do not kick your horse's sides, and do not pull hard on the reins, as this will hurt its mouth.

PET POINT

Your horse will get to know your smell and your voice. Talk quietly to your horse every time you see it.

24

Body Talk

A horse can communicate many different feelings—fear, anger, nervousness, curiosity and excitement—through its body.

When it is frightened or angry, a horse will flatten its ears and swish its tail from side to side. When it is happy, it raises its tail and points its ears forward.

▲ This Arabian horse has perked up its ears and raised its tail to show that it is happy as it runs around.

Sounds

Horses make many different sounds, which all have a meaning. They can **whinny**, neigh, snort, squeal, and cry. A horse will neigh—a loud sound a bit like an announcement—to tell other horses that it is there.

▲ The white horse has its ears back and is neighing to warn the other horse to stay away.

Instant Expert

Horses are mammals. Mammals are animals that are covered in hair and feed their young with milk.

The Largest

The largest horse ever is thought to be a shire horse named Mammoth. He was born in 1848, and stood 21.2 hands—about 7.2 ft. (2.2 m)—high. He weighed about 3,300 lb. (1,500 kg).

▼ Shire horses are heavy horses. They are tall and strong, but they are also very gentle.

The Smallest

The smallest horse is a miniature horse called Thumbelina. She is just 17 in. (43 cm) tall and weighs 57.3 lb. (26 kg).

The Oldest

The oldest horse ever is believed to have been one called Old Billy that lived in the 19th century. He lived to be 62 years old.

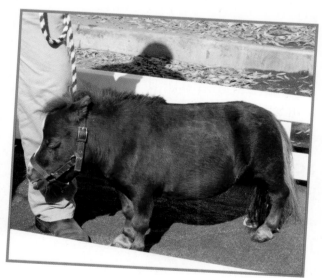

▲ Thumbelina, a dwarf miniature chestnut mare, is smaller than many pet dogs.

Sleeping Horses

Horses are able to sleep standing up because of the **tendons** and **ligaments** around their kneecaps. When a horse wants to sleep, these lock its legs in position so it can relax without falling over. This means the horse does not have to struggle to its feet if a predator creeps up on it.

◄ Brumby horses in Australia live in the wild **outback**.

Spirit Horses

The Mongolians call Przewalski horses *takhi*, which means spirit. They were given this name because these horses are fierce and impossible to ride. Mongolians believe that no one has ever been able to ride a Przewalski other than Genghis Khan, the famous Mongol leader who lived 800 years ago.

pet Quiz

Now that you know a bit more about what is involved in looking after a horse, is a horse the right pet for you?

1. Do you have lots of free time to look after your pet?
- **a)** No, I have lots to do
- **b)** I can get up early to see my horse and spend time with it after school and on weekends
- **c)** I can spare a bit of time in the evening

2. When should you groom your horse?
- **a)** Never, they don't need grooming
- **b)** Several times a week, and always before you ride
- **c)** Only when they get dirty

3. How long should you leave between feeding and exercising or riding your horse?
- **a)** You can ride right away
- **b)** About an hour
- **c)** 30 minutes

4. How often do you need to muck out a horse's stable?
- **a)** Once a month
- **b)** Every day
- **c)** About once a week

5. How long, on average, does a horse live?
- **a)** 5 years
- **b)** 25 years or more
- **c)** 15 years

Pet Quiz - Results

If you answered (b) to most of the questions, then a horse could be for you.

Owning a Pet: Checklist

All pets need to be treated with respect. Remember, your pet can feel pain and distress.

To be a good pet owner you should remember these five rules. Make sure your pet:

- never suffers from fear and distress
- is never hungry or thirsty
- never suffers discomfort
- is free from pain, injury, and disease
- has freedom to show its normal behavior

You should check your horse twice a day to make sure it has enough fresh water and food. Remember to order new supplies of its food in plenty of time so that your pet never goes hungry. If you can't do this every day, you must make sure there is someone who will.

You must keep your horse's stable clean, and make sure that the horse has enough room to move around. Check its paddock to make sure there is nothing there that may hurt it. The paddock must have a fence that is secure so your horse cannot escape.

Horses live in groups and can get lonely, so your pet must share a paddock with another animal, such as a horse, donkey, or goat. Give your horse plenty of exercise. If your horse becomes ill or hurts itself, tell a grown-up and get it checked by a vet immediately.

Glossary

bit a piece of metal that is part of the bridle; it is placed in a horse's mouth.

blind spot an area where a horse cannot see

bred the careful selection of parents to produce young with special features

breeds special types of horses which have certain features, for example an Arabian

captivity being confined; for example, when an animal is kept by people on a farm or in a zoo

domesticated tamed by people

dressage riding and training a horse to show off its balance, obedience, and athletic abilities

farrier a person who trims and fits horse shoes

fencer the device that powers and controls an electric fence

feral animals that were once tame but are now living wild

foal a young horse of either sex under a year old

girth a strap that goes around a horse's body to keep the saddle in place

grooming cleaning and brushing a horse's coat to remove dirt

halter a strap that fits around the head of a horse

laminitis a swelling inside the hoof of horse; it causes the horse to become lame and unable to walk properly.

ligaments tough but flexible straps of tissue that hold two bones together at a joint, for example around the elbow or knee

livery yard stables where horses are looked after for their owners

lunge line a long lead made of leather or webbing used for training or exercising a horse

manger an open container that holds hay for horses to feed from

mare female horse aged 4 years and older

mustangs feral horses that live in North America

outback remote and uninhabited regions, found especially in Australia

paddock a fenced field used to graze or exercise horses

predators animals that hunt and eat other animals for food

rodeos events where cowboys show their skills at riding

stallion a male horse over 4 years of age, still able to have offspring

suckle to feed on milk from the mother

tendon tough tissue that holds joints in place

whinny a soft, gentle neighing sound made by a horse

withers the tallest point of a horse's body formed by a ridge between the shoulder blades

Websites

Animal Planet offers a Horse Guide from A to Z, Horse Games, information on how to train and care for a horse, and more!
http://animal.discovery.com/guides/horses/horses.html

Learn more about the history of wild horses in America.
http://www.mustangs4us.com/mustang4.htm

Learn about horses at National Geographic.
http://animals.nationalgeographic.com/animals/mammals/horse/

Index